The Forbidden Door

The Selected Poetry of Lasse Söderberg

translated by Lars Gustaf Andersson & Carolyn Forché

ARROWSMITH
PRESS

The Forbidden Door:
The Selected Poems of Lasse Söderberg

ISBN: 979-8-9863401-1-1

Boston — New York — San Francisco — Baghdad
San Juan — Kyiv — Istanbul — Santiago, Chile
Beijing — Paris — London — Cairo — Madrid
Milan — Melbourne — Jerusalem — Darfur

11 Chestnut St.
Medford, MA 02155

arrowsmithpress@gmail.com
www.arrowsmithpress.com

The Forty-Fourth Arrowsmith book
was typeset & designed by Ezra Fox
for Askold Melnyczuk & Alex Johnson
in Garamond and Palatino Linotype fonts

Cover art: *Middle Path*, Liz Hawkes deNiord
36"x36" acrylic and gold leaf on canvas
Photographed by Rachel Portesi

The Forbidden Door

The Selected Poetry of Lasse Söderberg

translated by Lars Gustaf Andersson & Carolyn Forché

CONTENTS

from En dörr med lås (A door with a lock, 1965)

from De söndervittrade (The mouldered, 1965)

from Generalens måltid och andra dikter (The meal of the General and other poems, 1969)

from Ros för en revolution (A rose for a revolution, 1972)

from Undrens tid (Age of wonder, 1974)

from Slottet La Coste ligger in ruiner (The Castle La Coste is in ruins, 1989)

from Småsten till pyramiden (Pebbles for the pyramide, 1989)

from Sexton dikter (Sixteen poems, 1991)

from Pilar mot månen (Arrows towards the moon, 1992)

from Ögonen och minnet (The eyes and the memory, 1993)

from Europas snäcka (The shell of Europa, 2001)

from Stenarna i Jerusalem (The stones of Jerusalem, 2002)

from Jorden är blå (The Earth is blue, 2011)

from En svart vind blåser (A black wind blows, 2016)

from Den som ingenting vet
(The one who knows nothing, 2016)

from Frågor om historien (Questions about the history, 2017)

INTRODUCTION

As the Swedish poet Lasse Söderberg enters his ninth decade, we are honored to bring this selection of his poetry to readers of English for the first time, gathering almost seventy years of lyric art in a single volume. Many factors contributed to the belatedness of this translation, but perhaps foremost among them is Söderberg's dedication to the work of others rather than to promotion of his own; to the spirited international conversation of poets, to engagement with the world, with art and politics, to the celebration of poetry as "event" in the commons: a public, emancipatory art. The festivals and "happenings" he organized throughout his life drew future Nobel Laureates together with amateurs, the self-taught and the formally educated. Most importantly, they attracted the interest of people from every walk of life. He recognized early the dangers of confining poetry to the academy, and to the printed page, and he wanted to break free, an impulse that was unwittingly ignited in childhood by his father who, despairing of his son's lack of interest in academic work, sent him away to a boarding school in France.

What his father did not foresee was that Söderberg would be drawn to contemporary French poetry rather than rote learning. He would gravitate toward the Surrealists, with their wild explorations of the human imagination. He was not destined ever to complete his formal education, but instead set off to travel, first all over Europe, living principally in France and Spain, and then throughout Latin America. He wrote and lived restlessly, moving between countries and languages, mastering Spanish and French, along with sufficient Dutch, Danish, German, English, and Italian to become the foremost translator of post-war contemporary poetry into Swedish. He created a home in his native language for such poets as Octavio Paz, Seamus Heaney, Adonis, Derek Walcott and most recently, Jorge Luis Borges. He also translated the Americans: Charles Simic, Donald Hall, Robert Bly.

This work of bringing poets together, and translating their poetry into Swedish, was duly acknowledged with awards and stipends, and even (against his wishes), the conferral of a Professorship awarded by the Swedish government. But although he published at least thirty books of poetry, as well as chapbooks and limited editions, exhibition catalogues and collaborations with visual artists, his poetry was never given its due. The only poet of his generation to be fully recognized internationally was Tomas Tranströmer, whom Söderberg knew and whose work he admired, although after Stockholm, their poetics diverged. Tranströmer, situated within the academy, developed a strong interest in Christian mysticism, while Söderberg, a free spirit, traveled restlessly, cultivating the erotic imagination.

Söderberg was the Swedish poet closest to the Surrealist group in Paris. The language of his early poems, especially the chapbooks produced in the early fifties as part of the avant-garde group "Metamorfos," were characterized by a highly associative language struggling against conventional norms. By 1955, however, he had developed a much sparer, clearer style, while preserving the Surrealists' interest in metaphor.

Scholars and critics have noted a period of silence in the career of Söderberg between 1972 and 1989, during which he published no poetry books of his own, but turned his attention to travels, translation, and the launching of a poetry festival in Sweden, which brought poets from all over the world to Malmö, a southern town far from Stockholm. In 1989, Söderberg published two books of poems notable for their simplicity and lightness of touch, notes from an ongoing journey. His works continued to address the subjects of life and death, formulating a critique of civilization, most especially its religions and gods. He traveled to Jerusalem and Bagdad, Andalusia and Nicaragua, witnessing corruption and violence, all the while preserving his characteristic hopefulness, albeit in an ironic vein. He is a poet of presence and close attention. For him, to be within poetry to is to be attentive toward everything that happens, including political life. He opposed the American war in Vietnam, and condemned the dictatorships in Latin America and Spain (where he had lived under the regime of General Franco). He has also been in constant dialogue with music and other art forms, ever inventing ways in which poetry could be alive in the public sphere, through cabaret, jazz ensembles and poetry recitations. He organized and wrote catalogues for visual art exhibitions, and included poetry readings on opening nights.

Throughout his life, Lasse Söderberg has devoted himself to poetry, with imagination and grace. He has helped a host of poets to be read and heard in Swedish, but has always maintained a quiet reticence toward furthering his own work's reception in the world. If he was waiting for the time when the world of poetry would return his generosity of spirit, we hope that moment has come.

Lars Gustaf Andersson and Carolyn Forché
Lund, Sweden, May 2022

Paul Eluard in memoriam

Can the urn be more beautiful than the water?
Can the death of a poet light up the world?

The day was mother-of-pearl, it was the most beautiful day
that winter.
A horse made of light trampled the sky.
A letter arrived from the emptiness
and a bell of snow shattered with a clear sound.

Listen to light words hum on the lips of a poem.
Listen to their heartbeat, the simple force of a fountain.
A lantern of straw swings in our magical garden:
there is someone studying thoroughly the heraldry of fruits.

Waters of heaven, metro station, suburb tightened like a chest!
Someone has died in Paris, in the city of his many births,
under the sun of hope, under the love that has withered away.
A sick dog is lurking outside the door.

I see you: wise one with thoughts of light both nervous
and transparent, see you dissolve to dust,
see you drift away as thin smoke or snow,
a cloud of black snow on white nights.

Farewell to childhood

We escaped from school on a day when the clouds were hanging low.
Deep summer woods were our secret refuge.
Among nettles and pheasants, we dreamed great
catastrophes, fantasy cities, princely fortunes.

The world was always glass, there were hedges
around every garden, but overwhelmed by childish de-
light we raced into the silence. One day
we woke in a field outside time.

Small rivers coursed in our fingers, girls with pale bodies
played between airy trees, ships heavy with joy
sailed through the classroom windows, toward endless
adventures, toward a sky of moss from the ice age.

Then we ran away from our frost-bitten dreams
from clothbound books and the shadow of the teacher
towards another, larger shadow. Now we are throwing our arms
back without finding anything, out in an emptiness of memories.

(for Dennis Creffield)

FROM FÅGELN I HANDEN
(THE BIRD IN THE HAND, 1959)

For Tomas Tranströmer

(after reading 17 poems once again)

You know the broken history of things,
the alchemy of stones, a world masked
in the blind light of God. See how the summer dust rises
                        among the bones of the dead.

And you know the direction of the bird flocks.
You are standing in the wandering light of the secret
and into the heart flows our poor language.
                        The image is your salt.

You pass the fog in the north. Mountain.
The vulture's eye-view. Over the whole earth
the geography trembles. The clearings of clarity
                        are open everywhere.

The rain is, of course, a longer poem.
But where the elements are widening,
your Swedish narrows. And in the outer archipelago of the soul
                        the branch of the poem is swaying.

Ways

I'm holding a bird in my hand
but I don't know if it is alive.
A strange lightness: a song
transformed into a deceptive body.

The way of school children was the wing
that lifted in the time of winds.
My way goes down below, in the ravine
where the bird fell soundlessly.

A glass of water

A glass of water is shimmering in your hand:
a first spring which is taken by surprise,
a little definition of that clarity
which never vanishes from the world.

A glass of water: a wind with no north,
a circle as perfect as our day.
You drink. And on your sad lips
a happy light already shines.

FROM DET OBESTÄNDIGA
(THE IMPERMANENT, 1963)

The poet writes for the wind

for León Felipe

For whom does the poet write?
For everything that wanders and suffers,
everything that over and over is beaten to the ground
and disappears. For the grey stones
because they resemble humans.
For everyone and no one.

Jerez of the Border

1.

The last darkness. The south
is shivering in the nightshirt of mists.
Almond trees and windmills appear,
angels evil or good.

2.

A man stops himself on the corner,
paralyzed by bells and fear.
The ground burns under his feet:
hell flames and quivers.

3.

Processions are making their way through the city
led by the racket of the priest.
Tears and candles gleam faintly
in the haze of the outcasts.

4.

Remorse: a single wall.

5.

It is six o'clock in the morning.
I'm waiting for a bus and I hear
the voices of the abyss scorn
those who live, those who suffer.

The sky over Fresnes

All winter I have seen
the sky over Fresnes, grey and dirty
like the walls where someone stayed
to be judged by the stones.

All winter I have walked
on empty streets and thought that the sky
looked like a damp rag that someone
desperately presses to a mouth,

All winter, wrapped in melancholy
by the high bird-flecked wall
I have appealed to the light shimmering
out of the unbearable wound

The words that I dream about

The words that I dream about
are wingtips in the language
cinnabar on fine brushes
or wheat sheaves that tickle the wind.

But also:
the glistening of knives,
folds of mourning clothes worn from use,
discouragement in large cities.

The words I dream about
do not neutralize each other,
they can never even be read
from the lines in the palm.

The words I dream about
live in everything that ignites unrest:
bruises, bloodstains, nipples
and the flipsides of medals.

The words that I dream about
are the quickening of the poem.
On the lips of mercy silent outcries
and metaphors linger.

Poplars

One morning, once again
among blind grazing stones
and flute-player-shadows
the high poplars of the plains,

The leaves are restless.
And the trucks are reaching as
if they were to write. What?
Nothing. Infinite nothing.

I want to be among them
to share their weightless unrest, sink
deep among their roots
and shout:

—Poplars, you follow me
along rivers filled with clouds,
you follow me, filled with coolness,
poplars, high in the wind!

FROM EN DÖRR MED LÅS

(A DOOR WITH A LOCK, 1965)

To language

Cow parsley on a summer night,
pale sisters, I beg you
to shine in my distant voice,
I beg you to be my lamp,
my silent lamp that lays bare
the bird feather in the fist
of the schoolboy, the keys
in the spring, the toss of dice
within every quiet syllable.
Your meekness spurs me
along distant slopes of a ditch
and is no longer meekness
when I'm running, but drift
off in the cradle of the nine vowels.

In Lope de Vega's house

The stairwell in his house blackens
as a shadow under low windows
and the copper of the brazier
no longer reflects his head or the children's.
The guests have fallen asleep. The heart wanders,
blinded as before among furniture, memories,
books, while the pen rasps
like a wing feather
or maybe some mistress breathes beyond the words
close to the yard's
only orange tree. As balm
for his pain, honey for his lips,
are the songs of the people when slowly
he approaches the iced streams of his winter.

The forbidden door

1.

No one has lost the key
to the forbidden door.
Do not look for it.
Do not try to break in.
No one has lost the key.
It flows like water.
It is heavy as a stone.
It is one with the hand.
As volatile as one
with it as a gesture.
No one has lost the key.
Do not look for it.
In the grass that subdues us
it gives its answer.

2.

On both sides of the door
there is the same uncertainty.
See through the keyhole:
Do you look in or out?
Is a sky spreading out
over an open country
with these unspeakably simple
truths like fruits?
Is there a refuge,
a room with books,
lit lamps, identical time?
Do not expect answers.
First you have to ask
the right questions.

3.

The forbidden door
is the unyielding wall
before you.
Behind it you can hear
the sound of someone running away
and a strange wailing
(maybe your own)
while in vain you
look for the doorknob.
Do not try to break in.
The only thing you can
stick to is this:
on both sides of the door
the door is closed.

The poet in April

Today I have seen hunger
prowl round about, César Vallejo!
In your electrifying patience
it was a beast. It crawled
through you, devoured you from within,
broke into your shut mouth.
It could never be mine,
at least not in the same way.
I just saw it prowl around,
grey she-wolf of humanity,
with dried teats on fire,
under the whining bone of the month,
under the earthly chain of wailing,
under these hand-loose poems.

The dead children in the Tajo River

They have left the city
and their blind games
under the white bone of the sun,
they have left the voices
that called on the beach
and were once theirs.
Now they listen in the mud
to the river that plays
its slow trombone.
Now they dream without eyes
among lost things:
a tin can, a bottle,
a mule that slowly comes down
to the water to drink.

Sunspot in the grass

I am still among you
silent objects and eyelids,
you objects that I am close to
when swarms of frightened starlings
lift from my heart.
I am still living among you,
you silent objects close to
the buzzing lamp of summer,
when nameless friends leaned
over smoking herbaria.
Brooding within yourselves
you see everything snatched away.
But the day fills my gaze
and doesn't allow me to cry.

FROM DE SÖNDERVITTRADE
(THE MOLDERED, 1965)

The moldered

The ones who leave us have won. Dark, silenced, they approach in a windless place. They no longer resemble us in their resolute bishop chairs. Instead it is we who resemble them.

*

When I walk to meet them I come to a wall. It is low, the height of a man, with marks of bullet holes and tears. What is the point of pounding my knuckles bloody against it? I will not go further. I stand by the wall and smell the burning stench of life.

*

The panther breathes nightly beneath the temporal bone. It crouches as if in a dream and waits a long time in that position, turned inwards. When it finally dares to jump, its fur is already burning and its eyes are empty. Behold the skeleton of the air!

*

Clarity, do not walk out on me under the unyielding bone. Do not walk out on me. I will raise you like a lamp over the poverty of the stones.

*

Let me linger a while by this window facing the last clearing. All windows in one! The lull makes it close. It scents the light.

*

The ones who leave us have won. I give them one word: abomination. Their beauty is dark. They are stumbling in their ravines. And I know that there always will be a blind spot within us: their bitter moon.

FROM GENERALENS MÅLTID
OCH ANDRA DIKTER

(THE MEAL OF THE GENERAL
AND OTHER POEMS, 1969)

With heart-chalk

What has happened with your America,
Walt Whitman? What has become
of the strong love that you celebrated
and the institutions you distrusted?
You, tender spokesman of democracy,
what has happened to your sons?
Under the tutelage of the technocrats
they are rolling in the stench of gold
and are swallowed up by the latrines
of race hatred where white tape-worms feast.
Your America is no longer yours.
Therefore I will, without hesitation,
write over your name Walt Whitman,
with heart-chalk the word Vietnam.

FROM ROS FÖR EN REVOLUTION
(A ROSE FOR A REVOLUTION, 1972)

At daybreak

The nights of stained velvet
have stolen away from the houses,
rustling like green banknotes
that have whirled all the way to Miami.
The moon is left like a token
from a confiscated slot machine.

Havana 7:00 p.m.

1.

The fifth precinct
is no longer a police station,
just an empty house with boards
over windows and doors.

2.

Outside some kids are playing
in the weeds
without a thought of the executioners
and their gruesome nights.

3.

Never have I been
farther from death than now!
When the wind of nightfall blows,
it is filled with hidden lovers.

From one reality to another

Cattle
with horns like long curves in a signature
graze daylight from the fields.

The royal palms
are ink pens falling from the sky
and stabbing the ground.

In a shadow,
the only ink on the landscape, serious men sit

and learn to write.

Guayabera

The wind loves the white clouds
that are hung to dry on the sky,
the white geese that are born and die
in the green twilight,
the white shirts, stiff like paper
and inside a little fist
endlessly pounds on the door of being.

A part of America

(Guantánamo)

Airplanes lift and land all the time.
A battleship steams in the heat.
The landscape is like sheet metal.

There no fly will rest.
There soldiers are on guard
in towers and sniper nests.

They are watching us in their field glasses.
We are watching them in our field glasses.
The heat between us waits and waits.

FROM UNDRENS TID
(AGE OF WONDER, 1974)

Message from Theseus

Nowadays the labyrinth lies up-lit, crisscrossed by escalators and elevators that make the walk more comfortable than it was. It is not difficult to get around. But despite this I cannot find my way out of this maze. I have lost my thread, it is cut off, as long as I can remember it has been cut off, and while I look for it in the tile-clad corridors I hear gynecologists' shears continually working under fluorescent lights. Of the Minotaur, not a trace.

FROM SLOTTET LA COSTE LIGGER IN RUINER
(THE CASTLE LA COSTE IS IN RUINS, 1989)

Alejandra

She collected dry grass between the cobblestones so as to make a small fire. She collected straws of hay from the hair of those passing by. She collected sticks that had fallen from the high ballroom windows where shadows moved back and forth to the music of waltzes dressed in mourning clothes. She collected tears from the trees. All of this she threw on the fire. It burned a short while, hardly enough to warm her fingers. Then she held the mirror of ashes to herself and saw how much she resembled the fire that has gone out.

Lilith's Rest

1

Her hair grows while she sleeps, as it grows on the dead. Her hair is black as the river of death. In its swirls you can make out a pale face with closed eyes and the mouth open in a cry for help. Or is it in accusation? Who knows. Those who drown don't ask.

2

Between her spread legs the desert sand is flowing. The lizards slither away in fear when she moves. In her hand she holds some charred seeds she will give to the man when he pines away. Their total number provides the solution to her riddle.

3

The moon is her mirror. There she beholds her nakedness, as when you are looking at a tower in ruins . In her vicinity the flashes stop, the welding flames freeze into ice. But her eyes burn through a veil of sorrow.

4

Anus is the third eye.

The unmade bed

Already a memory, clouds over the battlefield on Armistice Day. Dawn came washing through the marble quarries. The roads wound empty through a deserted place. Ahead of me I saw the white riverbed from which the dark water of the night had flowed out, whirling and sighing. On the pillow, where the head of the water nymph had been resting, there was now only the scar of a monogram.

White, she thinks

The wheel tracks: lifelines of a landscape. They end here, maybe because of the hard frozen ground, or because the road, as far as one can see, goes no further.

Thin snow whirls in through the open car door. She has got out and has walked over to the driver clad in black who stands smoking some steps away. They could not have chosen a more hopeless place. In his glasses she can see reflected the naked trees. The look like bony thighs, growing out of the ground.

It is not the imagination that gives her gooseflesh. Behind them is the car, still with the door open for the journey to nowhere. He is the Ferryman who draws a last smoke and tosses the cigarette before leaning towards her. Close to her ear she can hear his wristwatch tick, as if their barely living tableau were time itself delayed. White, she thinks. White. Can fire freeze?

FROM SMÅSTEN TILL PYRAMIDEN
(PEBBLES FOR THE PYRAMID, 1989)

Written in stars

A book with black pages
is the star-smeared heaven.

Every night a page is turned
before our puzzled eyes.

The text is always the same,
a sparkling of raised Braille.

*

I walked through the park in Chaltultepec
where the coyote paces in his cage.

He stops, cranes his neck, whines
under the star of his confinement.

That which lights my way through the park
 is indifferent to his destiny.

*

Everyman who wants to know
will get a fistful of salt in the eye.

Better then to look down
on the hard ground beneath our feet.

If images exist somewhere, they are there,
omens to be read.

*

In the clay pit a star sees itself.
It moves.

*

Destiny is blind, say the old
and they never turn the page back.

Nothing can be changed
and nothing is unchangeable.

Our own whirlwind of debris
is definitive, circling, uncertain.

*

During the day, Indian women
sell food for the journey by the roadside:

bits from heaven wrapped in green leaves,
biscuits baked with star flour

which for us born later has a taste of time
kneaded for thousands of years.

And the eyes of the vendors
are the constellations of earth.

The Grass in Managua

1
A herd of ruins were grazing
in the middle of town, I thought.

Grass grew there like the hair of the dead.
It had its story to tell.

I sat down and listened
as if for the first time.

Children approached empty-handed,
their fathers taken away from them, dark.

They resembled the burnt grass
below which the new grass will come.

There were also men and women,
silent, serious as roots.

They all listened, I thought
as if for the first time.

2

The place where I was
was an interval, overgrown,

the turning point between two times
that both existed,

one of them without a real beginning,
the other without a real end

and in the same way I was
at my own turning point

where I was cleaved in two
both strangers to each other

and still living in the same breath.
But here, between born and unborn,

I was an impermanent witness,
a grass myself among the ruins.

3

That which was nothing, becomes.
That which became nothing, is.

Whispers quickly scribbled
in the grass went back to obscurity.

Here and there were small stones
like turds the ruins dropped,

those who had slowly wandered away
I thought while the men,

the women and children were left
without moving, resolute

like the prison bars of silence,
armed with their forbearance.

The ash that I saw in their hands
was the birth of a country.

A small trip to heaven

to C.O. Hultén

During my walk through the country of morning, I arrived at last at the place where the whirling dead leaves finally gather to be reborn. There was a wonderful elastic building without beams or walls, a kind of cage without bars which did not rest firmly on the ground but glided over it as blue music. I stopped with wonder, let go of my earthly burden. What a flutter of wings! What craned necks! What green cries! Even I thought for a moment that I was changed, could be taken up with the leaves and danced around before they, as if by happy coincidence, flew up to decorate the trees with their song.

In the Willow Pond Park

1.
I'm sitting in the shadow of the tree.
The afternoon break in the green grass
stretches out beyond me.

I sit in the organ music made of light
and have to close my ears
to catch this flickering concert.

Things cast and trees give shadow .
The shadow doesn't get up and walk away.
My shadow sits down, absorbed.

2.
The one who sits under a tree
doesn't think about that tree
as if it were someone close

and when he sits there
doesn't see all trees in the world
as one bustling family,

he himself belongs to dead things
that cast dead shadows.
He is in the treelessness.

3.

Now the light is on its last stanza.
When the resting hour darkens
the shadow gives off its scents.

An obscure unrest.
It gleams like hard nails
in there. But I stay put.

The tree breathes in, the shadow breathes out.
If there were no trees,
we wouldn't dare to die.

Organer grinder

(Amsterdam)

1.
Why read the newspaper
when the pigeons don't?
The breaking news of the day:
a girl in a flowery dress
walks across a bridge.

2.
Three kinds of bustling:
the organ music that rises around her,
the sunlight swarming in the canal
and the pigeons out of step
with the marching music.

3.
I put away the paper
and walk myself across the bridge.
The air is like gold leaf.
I take a deep breath
and become as gilded inside.

The train stops

When the train suddenly halts there on the tracks, between two stations, the cars are filled with a silence that, for a short moment, confuses us. This is the silence before the time of machines, maybe before the time of man and the great mammals too mammoth for us where we sit with our faces pressed to the cold windows so as to see something we recognize out there in the darkness, beyond our own reflections. We wait. When the cars again, and again all of a sudden, start moving, we turn our faces toward the lighted corridors. On the whole train it is only the drinking water in the glass pitcher that tries to keep at least a measure of the silence, trembling with irritation in its metal cage. In vain: the moment is already past.

Five copper pennies

for Octavio Paz

(Kåseberga)

Grass, sea and heaven:
the same kind of deep joy
to write and to see.

(Baltic Sea haiku)

Between the fingers
time runs without moving:
a necklace of amber.

(Gulls)

While we talk
gulls appear as commas
in the wind from the southeast.

(Ancient remains)

The sky sapphire blue.
But the clouds from long ago
are reflected in her eyes.

(At the picnic spot)

Here we are, tiller man!
The ship with its cargo of light.
Before us: summer.

FROM PILAR MOT MÅNEN
(ARROWS TOWARDS THE MOON, 1992)

With Jorge Guillén

Paseo Marítimo, 29

He builds joy. His life's work
soon finished. As when
sea and heaven meld together
in a sun-drunk shimmering.

The balcony door open. Air
out there. And a glimmer of water
that the old one in his chair
still in wonder, beholds.

From the ninth floor
as if from the height of nine decades
he sees the world as radiant:
sky and heaven together.

His life ends in this light
apparently without shadow.
Clarity, nothing else.
It is under the trees that the shadow waits.

FROM ÖGONEN OCH MINNET
(THE EYES AND THE MEMORY, 1993)

I walked along the wall,
built of dead hours.

That which I say, I conceal.
That which I conceal, I see.

A wall in unchanging light.
The name of the street: secret.

(blue)

Nowhere a key,
only doors.

Mirrors of sand
put the present moment at peace.

Unchanging light.
The heavenly dust of marble statues.

(labyrinth)

When I was about to leave,
I was held back by the word "out".

I turned around, always prepared,
in a labyrinth of my own.

When I was about to enter
I was held back by the word "in".

(magic in white)

Nothing here and
nothing there.

A cloud sails
into a closet.

May I present:
A quadrangular zero?

I have my eyes filled with earth, that is why
I can see clearly, nothing eludes me.

I have my hands filled with straw and clay,
this is the beginning of the end, nothing remains.

I have my head full of transparent scars.
The thoughts that have been inflicted upon me.

No one approaches me.
I can see this clearly.

No one is here.
No one speaks to me.

No one opens the door,
inviting me in.

FROM EUROPAS SNÄCKA
(THE SHELL OF EUROPA, 2001)

The well

He who wants to remember, and is full of darkness himself, must stand by the brim of himself as by a well,

he must lean over the well with a stone in his hand and ask himself what the well hides, how deep it is, how distant the light that reaches him,

and he must, to be able to know the depth and the darkness of the well, throw the stone and see it slowly fall, as if thoughtfully, as if hanging in empty nothingness, until it is no longer seen

and he remains standing and waits by the brim of himself, leaning forward, until the stone hits the hitherto invisible water's surface

and he who wants to remember can see how the deep suddenly sparks, attracts the light, becomes living as when an eye opens, and he is recognized by another eye below.

Hunger

J'allais sous le ciel, Muse! et j'etais ton féal.

Did I ever feel hunger? On the road in Europe, yes, sometimes
I think I felt hunger. Europe was filled with hunger.

I don't mean the hunger that wandered through the world like
a skeleton with metal cutlery.

I don't mean the hunger for love, the whirlpool that refills itself
or even the hunger for words, the miracle that sustains me.

I mean the hunger that is turned away, the one that doesn't tear
in the belly or in the heart or in the soul,

the hunger for stones and oblivion:

the stones that lie still on the same place and stay silent
and therefore are outside time,

the stones, scattered around, not knowing about each other, and in spite of all
fulfill the mission they once had

and oblivion, the only thing that is offered the one who knows that there is no
Cretan princess waiting,

oblivion as the natural condition, ashes to read, dust
in love, bird skeletons.

It was like wanting to go to a cloister, but a cloister without God,
a cloister white as an unwritten page,

outside, and filled with silence. There I would drink
of the light and eat of the shadow.

That hunger has never left me.

The snakes

On the slope of the mountain there were small sand-colored snakes that you could hear escape, rattling into the dry brush but they were not dangerous, nothing compared to the reptiles, nurtured by the hearts of the post-woman, the cab driver and the priest.

The post-woman had a boiling saucepan in her house, in the steam of it she opened all suspicious letters.

The cabdriver had a gun hidden under his seat, it would protect him against the angel of vengeance.

The priest wanted to stick his crucifix in the ass of the devil.

When I heard the small snakes rattle in the dry brush, I felt gratitude for them. They were more like the fear that crawled away in the hearts of the stonemason, the fisherman and the village idiot.

The mason speaks

Here is my hand. It is not of plaster though it is covered with mortar and dust. I know that it can bleed.

When my friends arrive I say nothing. I just reach out my hand to them.

The fisherman speaks

I had a boat that served me long and faithfully. She grazed starlight at sea, and mooed with joy when she returned home. Around her lamp my thoughts swarmed. I, who forget nothing, have yet forgotten her way.

I had a house that was steady in all weathers. It was built with bricks and confidence. The brazier was the red heart around which the family gathered. But I, who forget nothing, have forgotten where the house stood.

I had a daughter who gave joy as refreshing as the water in the jug, the one I have by the door through which she left. I, who forget nothing, have forgotten her name.

And I understand that I, though I forget nothing, now forget myself.

The village idiot speaks

I do not live at the place where I sleep. I live in the baptismal font. In the swaying of the boat where it is moored. Between the thighs of my mother.

On the damp hay mattress in a partition between the bone-house and the pig-stie I sleep.

Beside me are my gym shoes, yawning. I only speak English with them. To the inner walls, to the braces and to the neighbors I speak our own language. If they should want it I would speak English even with them.

No stones fly. But my shaved head flew when it came rolling to my shoulders.

When I do not sleep I see life go on. I am part of it. That is why I chew and swallow. When I do not chew and swallow it is because I sleep or am dead. When I am not dead I am a man.

The fig tree

The September light smelled of figs! It enveloped me. It was if as I had hidden deeply among the mysterious clothes in her wardrobe

while she stripped naked in the light and ran over the field, her hands blue with juice.

It was in the shadow of the tree where I hid. From there I could observe her and imagine that she even smelled like the September light, when it ripens.

*

How I have loved these fruits, turning blue like pain, but inside filled with sweetness!

When I picked them from the fig tree branches or spread out them at the table to dry them I felt the light wetness, as if it were from the groin of Lilith,

and when I took them to my lips it was as if she gave me the ancient vertigo she had given to men throughout time, lost as they were in the ruins of the Pleasure Garden.

She searched for the man in his house, where the fig tree grew. She thought him a branch himself of that tree. It was sink or swim.
She searched for the man to put an end to the discord between them. It could only happen unannounced and only at night.

She searched for the man in his house with her mouth and hands. She searched for him in his bed. The wind tore at the branches. He wrote his white signature on her nudity. In the morning she greeted the fig tree.

*

The figs open: the dawn of flesh

FROM STENARNA I JERUSALEM
(THE STONES OF JERUSALEM, 2002)

When night falls in Jerusalem

When night falls in Jerusalem
everything becomes strangely still,

as when in a sand-colored light, one
slowly closes a heavy book, hard to read

where death is a collection of legends,
the ties of kinship spin cobwebs

and backward thoughts stand against forward promises
behind book covers of stone, the eyelids of God.

The stones of Jerusalem

A boy went and drew his finger along the wall
as if counting all the stones of the city.
How many? An overwhelming number.

A young man held a stone in his hand,
it didn't fit anywhere except just there,
just then, it had no part in the city.

An older man sat with closed eyes
as if he wanted to be one of the city stones.
No one could talk him out of it!

An old man put a stone in his mouth.
It would speak in his place.
It would pray his prayer.

The most distant place

The most distant place
is within reach,

yet we cannot reach it,
it is hardly bigger than a nutshell

when we go out, looking for it,
believing we have it in our hand,

its golden luster renders it chimerical:
a broken mirage.

*

The dust travels between centuries
without being carried by a wind.

It lies down on the ground
and rests there like an unlined hand

on a fevered brow.
It lies on the greenest leaves

and is yellow, like a disease.
The dust: time ground down.

*

Before the esplanade, empty of people,
on the top of the rock I think:

I am neither pilgrim nor prophet
and I will probably never be closer than this

to the grey dwelling of God.
As the confidant of the pebbles

and the poet in Jerusalem
my mission is of this world.

*

In the sky, time-honored clouds.
On the ground, stones with fight still left in them.

No humility anywhere.
No merciful night.

The most distant place
is the place that kills people.

May a drop of their blood
enter the rock.

*

On the Roman road
an old Arab walks by.

With his bundle on his back
he is a walking owner's mark.

In the bundle he carries petrified tears,
splinters from Sabra and Chatila.

The most distant place
is the one under his feet.

*

The weakness of one part
becomes a strength.

The strength of the other part
An unmistakable weakness.

Inside the stone
I imagine a seed.

It grows slowly.
Is it thus weak or strong?

*

The most distant place
always belongs to the other,

kneaded together by time and faith.
It is a petrified promise.

It is his own place
that the other has made his,

reinforced by all defeats.
Israel is an idea, built on humiliations.

When I walk through Jaffa Gate

... a due mie sensi
faceva dir l'un "No", l'altro "Sì, canta"

When I walk through Jaffa Gate
I leave behind a part of myself.

It is the incredulous part.
It stands there, pawing the ground.

The part I bring with me
when I walk through Jaffa Gate

is the one that wants to be devoured.
It hastens ahead, filled with expectation.

*

Thus deserted by these opposites
I become immobile inside.

All pleas are crushed against this intransigence
and fall helpless to the ground.

Yet I ask my indifferent limbs
and my encapsulated soul:

which gathering will be mine
when I walk through Jaffa Gate?

*

Which gathering will be mine,
Which market mine, which powers?

Shall I walk against the current
or shall I follow it?

Shall I mix with the holy
or with the unholy?

Shall I talk with the dead,
shall I see the living?

*

The living wait.
The dead act.

They do not know their place
under the parched laurel tree.

That is why they wander about without eyes
everywhere there are eyes

and when I walk through Jaffa Gate
I see what they once saw.

*

When I walk through Jaffa Gate
I am met by the shadow of great Herod

and the shadow of his three towers
that cast no shadow.

He still shouts out their names
over the nameless roofs

and still trembles, with his madness tattooed
inside his head.

*

A bit to the right, the eye of the needle.
But no camel is to be seen anymore.

A bit to the left, the grave,
shoveled from the inside.

Straight ahead, the wall
built with horror-struck stones.

Everything is closed. Walkers
hurry by without looking at each other.

*

Everything is closed, as hard mouths,
as scars, as blocked streets.

For security reasons?
Because of the present situation?

The long siege?
Or because of the great,

alas, all too great fatigue of the angels,
that find their rest between these houses?

*

In the dark, covered footpaths of the bazaar,
you find yourself walking in an underground city.

In the eternal city
the small shops are the most eternal.

The navel of God is a portal
where each and every one cries out in distress

Or their goods, their knick-knacks,
and all kinds of merchants' spices.

The smell of saffron and sandalwood
makes me human again.

*

In the bazaar I paid attention to the hard mixture of gold leaf and
blood, and the powdery, almost flickering consistency of the spice
supplied in one of the stalls. I turned over the container and looked for
a label that could say something about the content. The spice merchant
looked at me for a while and then approached. "What I sell here are
ground human souls", he said. "You can get them cheap in Jerusalem."

*

When I walk through Jaffa Gate
I explain to the stones:

I believe in the walking past
but not in the ignorance.

I believe in the traffic passing through,
in a country without permits.

As witness I call the desert lark,
the desert lark and the insects.

*

First the desert, then the labyrinth,
the old stones and the new ones,

the inland shell filled with the drone of history,
that God himself lifts up from the gravel

and holds to his ear to listen
to the spiral of complications:

A course a course a course of events
until the beginning is reached!

In my room at Mishkenot
I make my tea, I read my paper.

Many messages come to me.
No messages come from me.

I am flesh suffused with time
on a raft of light.

It is my flying carpet
which carries me where the words are.

FROM JORDEN ÄR BLÅ
(THE EARTH IS BLUE, 2011)

Sunset

(Granada)

The grass,
a burnt voice.

The well,
a broken pimpernel.

Heaven,
white clothes stained with blood.

The crime was committed here

(Viznar)

A black car
at the roadside.

An angel
without a face
among the trees.

The clock
is at five in the afternoon.

In the stillness
someone is crying:
the spring of Ainadamar.

      *

Stop,
time.

Two words
in the shadow's mouth.

And time
stopped.

An Elegy

I walked the guilt of my betrayal
along the friendly streets of Lisbon.
It was early on earth
but late in my lonely thought.

I was no one. The clothing was no one's.
In my pockets I had only crumbs of hope
and nothing more. There was a light breeze
as if an invisible door was open.

My shoes took me where they wanted.
But I put my melancholy
on a wobbly park bench in order to see
the wind playing with yesterday's paper.

The avenue was a sleeping muscle
or a measuring tape between then and now.
The light distributed leaflets under the trees.
No, not leaflets, it was withered leaves.

Once upon a time nightly patrols went by
and sounded like steel security gates drawn down.
Forbidden songs were hiding
in those who knew the deepest sorrow.

Then it became April.
And April was a rain of flowers
that let the petals of promises fall.
It was time to wake up.

The dead leaves hurried in one direction,
the bankers in another.
Otherwise it was empty. Two pigeons only:
like cobblestones wandering around.

Where were the dogs of Lisbon
with porcelain eyes and electrical paws?
Where were the cigars that dreamt
that they were Atlantic steam ships?

And where was the girl with the heavy braid
as black as the pillar of smoke from a factory stack?
Did she wait for me in the white villa
by the violet sea?

Was she still drinking the green wine?
Did she still read her Yeats
as if in confidence, able to quote:
no country for old men?

The paper fluttered to the ground
like a wing cut off.
Her eyes were glittering dark
as after a night's rain.

Ophelia, rose of spring, a sister
soaked, soaked and maybe drowned
in all the new sounds.
No pigeons cooing for the moment.

That which is early for some
is late for others.
In actual headlines!
Fading moments!

I was no one. My thought was no one's.
It was swept up with the rest of the garbage
with scraps of darkness
and with bits of wind.

The morning had changed
to a truth without lips,
empty, but filled with beginning.
And I thought:

early is far away from death,
late looks back and cries.
When I got up from the park bench
I let my melancholy stay there.

Cities

Ce sont des villes!

All my cities were imaginary,
cities in the mind, capital cities,
not different from dreams that you wake from
and try to remember.

All my cities were imaginary.
I walked on their streets accompanied
by ghosts that suddenly appeared
in the doorways to the houses where they had lived

or where I myself had been living
sometime, maybe long ago,
I had imaginary conversations full of
names and years with these fog beings

that I could be certain would appear
if only the city were imaginary enough.
Or were they friends in the real world
who still met me in those oases of stone

which were made of ideas more than stone
and whose imaginary past I shared?
Truly cities! To be lost in them
was to find yourself or parts of yourself

that you had forgotten or been unaware of:
streets that went in different directions,
flower markets and empty lots,
reality transformed into imagination.

All my cities were and continue to be
far away within me,
with buildings sensitive as eyelids.
It is in these that I live.

In Lisbon

(untitled)

Heaven is a white sail
filled with blue wind.
On board the city, I am
the admiral of Solitude

and the deck where I stand
is made of cobblestone.
I notice that it tilts.
Is it against you that it tilts?

In that case, it tilts downward.
As all those who are lost,
I adjust my gaze
and get my bearings.

I have worn my white linen shirt
to become one with the wind
and I wave my blue handkerchief
to become a piece of the sea.

All the men's hats have blown away.
All clocks are rushing ahead, restless,
and everybody here is a sailor
with the salt of melancholia in their blood.

The city pulls away from its moorings.
You can hear this in the poems of Pessoa.
Read them! The heart speaks in tongues there.
Language swells against the Atlantic piers.

I saw my heart lying
in a shop window in Chiado:
a red toy car made of tin
no one plays with any longer.

I wanted to give that to you
but you asked for roses and nightingales
bound together.
You were tired of worn-out toys.

Under the blue sail of sky
filled with white wind
I'm looking for roses,
I'm looking for nightingales.

The moon that Cervantes saw

(Alcalá de Henares)

The train stops. The moon that Cervantes saw
hangs over the low hill
as if an incunabulum, worn out from being read.

The moon is our reading lamp!
When the doors are closed and the train departs
the story can go on.

In the warm July night
cypress trees and supermarkets,
breweries and seats of learning pass slowly by.

To read Jabès in Jerusalem

1.

He didn't write
in order to have written.

He didn't come here
to be the one who he already was.

His long walk
took him through the book,

through language, back
to silence.

2.

He stayed living
in the house that he built,

just air,
and nonetheless stable on the ground of suffering,

only twilight
in the prismatic flux.

There he drank the waters of thought.
There he ate the bread of the word.

3.

The written is the frontispiece of the riddle.
The reverse side glows.

The written was already written
in the darkness between the lines,

Is it all song?
Is it all bone?

When all languages are forgotten
oblivion is over.

Mark Rothko

There are no answers
when you can't form the question.

I can't go further.
One threshold, several thresholds.

The last one, before me.
There is no God.

By the Damascus Gate

(Jerusalem)

From the doorway, I saw an outstretched hand.
A long time ago, a leprous man sat there.

It was as if he touched my forehead
and slowly said to me: "become another."

I didn't know what and who I was:
a seed, a pebble, a stream.

And who he was, one long since dead.
One who is now safe. One who has, possibly, returned.

     *

It was as if he touched my forehead.
Just a shadow. And everything was the same.

An ordinary day with people coming and going,
I was in the midst of them. I was and am.

Old cities are filled with sorrow,
new ones, with meaningless joy.

The old ones are wells
that give us darkness to drink

and darkness is meaning.
The new ones stand naked around us

and shout with naked voices
so loud that you hear nothing.

FROM EN SVART VIND BLÅSER
(A BLACK WIND BLOWS, 2016)

When I hear about the Syrian war

1.

When I hear about the Syrian war
my thoughts go to the house of Bashar Zarkan

in the nutmeg-colored Bab Toma
where all houses open inward.

It was as if they closed their eyes
to dream about wine and love making.

Now they are deserted. Sleeping dreamlessly
in the nutmeg-colored shadow.

2.

In my memory, I walk into the house,
finding my way, no one is there any longer,

the cool rooms have been plundered of voices,
the bed where I slumbered in the afternoon

is maybe covered in soot and ashes
as the inner courtyard by fallen lemons,

the tips of breasts that are no longer caressed.
Maybe all that is left of the well is thirst.

Fabiana

1.

I got lost in Harat al-Yahud,
the Jewish quarter.

Saw only walls, closed doors,
while the garden of pleasure was always within,

always secret, like our hotel room
that time, in a distant country.

There we locked ourselves in and played
"the first humans."

2.

The city was bustling outside
and in the noise we heard the peoples' protests

and the republic that was established.
A big moment.

It was thus in time we got lost
and not in space.

In spite of that we could not promise each other
anything except the next hour and the next.

3.

In Harat al-Yahud, the Jewish quarter,
there was no one to ask for directions.

I saw only walls, closed doors,
and all alleys had the same name.

If I walked in the direction of the time,
I said to myself, instead of in the direction of space,

I would surely find my way
between the closed door and the open one.

FROM DEN SOM INGENTING VET
(HE WHO KNOWS NOTHING, 2016)

The one who knows nothing

1.

In the forgotten valley
time seemed to be used up:

grass over words, gray
over green, stone over thought,

a crumbling wall
and the bell tower whose shadow

resembled a guillotine.
The insects nailed the moment.

2.

In the thickest undergrowth
the slowest belief.

The monastery, not part of nature
yet framed by nature,

silenced, half-deserted
under a circling black vulture.

Nonetheless, the old stone bridge bows politely
when strangers approach.

3.

Here sat the learned prior
with a quill pen in hand,

leaning over the beautiful, enigmatic stanzas
that a brother wrote in prison.

The words both troubled and confirmed,
troubled with beauty, confirmed with mystery.

The landscape creates the same impression here:
a garden of pleasure with thorns.

4.

In the grass, a discarded tin can,
dented and without a bottom.

The ant that crawls into the can
also crawls out.

If the ant realized this
she would be a student of Heraclitus.

Now she crawls in and crawls out
and doesn't know what it means.

5.

Cypresses, dark flames
that rise from the ground,

fearsome guards
in a row along the rock,

immobile sleepwalkers
in a world without mirrors,

you are drinking the prayers of the dead,
you are the exclamation marks of the dead!

6.

The wall of the rock: a palimpsest.
It demands seven learned men

to interpret the message,
and seventy years to understand it.

Truly,
a slow lesson!

If I had inner eyes,
I would read it.

7.

Cypresses and marble go together
in the world of the grave digger.

But near my feet
the creek is dancing with abandon.

It is as unabashedly naked as I am
where I sit on the naked rock.

The water has a god of its own
who is transparent, and laughs.

8.

The bumblebee can, as well as the helicopter,
hang in the air.

I listen to the bumblebee
as to an old acquaintance

before she flies off over the creek dissatisfied.
I haven't listened closely enough!

The water fleas are left, each one of them
performing its biblical miracle.

9.

The one who knows nothing
is happier than the one who knows.

Happiness is the absolute zero
vibrating in bumblebees and saints.

But the absolute zero in bumblebees
is not the absolute zero in saints.

Saints are not as happy as bumblebees.
They say that they know.

10.

The hermit deserted his name
so as to become no one.

He went into himself
as into a shining forest filled with empty questions.

Who am I?
Who am I not?

Everything is as before conception.
No traces of the three gods.

11.

As the hermit in his cave
I'm looking at my toenail

saying it is here.
The toenail is here and the foot

the toenail belongs to
and the whole rest of the body

which is the extension of the toenail.
The toenail is the beginning of the universe.

12.

He dreamed that he was
in the maze of the devil.

The walls were of flesh
and the blood pulsed

in the pale fretwork of the walls.
The nails were driven into the sighing flesh

until holy mists were covering everything.
The cooing of doves woke the hermit.

13.

The night, says Lope,
is the cave of thoughts.

When I walk into it
I hear the sound of wings and sighs.

I hear the clocks tick
in reality and in the walls.

I hear the death-clock tick,
the woodworm tick, matter tick.

14.

To draw yourself back into the idea
far away from the tumult,

is that the solution?
Is it enough to reject?

Vegetation is richer than gold,
the idea is the absence of the pulse in the stone.

Between vegetation and the idea
is a forked path.

15.

I am an invisible man
in the guise of a body,

he who gesticulates
without being understood,

the imaginary figure sitting here
on a rock in a gurgling creek

and thinks he is me,
visible until Sunday.

16.

Away from the people,
is that the solution?

Away from the herd
to the pebble stone?

Away from is
to not-is?

Away from Economy
to the drop of water?

17.

Economy is a scorpion
with a human face.

The drop of water, on the contrary,
hangs trembling over the deep

and will not fall—the hermit thinks.
Thus, it is slowly formed

into a transparent urn
holding timelessness.

18.

Buñuel overnights in Las Batuecas

To revolt against God
when there is no God is meaningful,

he thought, he who fell asleep
with Freud under his pillow.

Even scorpions have a love life,
he further thought.

Where there are no humans
there is no God.

19.

In the next cell: Eli Lotar,
a lost son of the avant-garde.

His sixteen-millimeter camera
was a scrutinizing eye

that hummed like the bumble bee
when he handled it.

Eli Lotar, a deserted name
flickering in the cinema darkness.

20.

The nightmare spills over
when it reaches the brim

and becomes many human lives
that swarm like piglets

on a bloody concrete floor
all naked, shimmering,

screaming like babies.

So many.
Far too many.

21.

On the mountain slope
villages like scabs.

Beehives with bitter honey,
flies that copulate.

Give up all hope!
There is no one to love.

Is that why the monastery
is called the desert by its inhabitants?

22.

"The forecourt of hell
and a taste of paradise

at one and the same time,"
says the traveler summing things up.

Half shit half gold.
Not even the alchemist

is able to annul the difference,
not even human love.

23.

In this forgotten valley
time seemed to be used up,

an empty shell
with a microscopic inscription,

an empty tin can
with an industrious ant,

all this purity,
see how it closes up on itself!

24.

The inscription says:
"Consider, that which was

never will be,
that nothing before is

and nothing after
and that which you read

and that which you write
you read and write

now."

FROM FRÅGOR OM HISTORIEN
(QUESTIONS ABOUT THE HISTORY, 2017)

With green ink

Neruda wrote with green ink.
On every page a thicket of emeralds.

Through the years it meandered
this literal vegetation.

Horses can be green!
No pleasure garden is blue!

With such a pen, he said to himself,
every doubt should go away.

Therefore: green ink,
lyric chlorophyll.

To Comala

1.

I arrived in Comala where everyone was dead. The starving dogs were also dead even though I could hear them bark. The bell in the church tower had stopped. On the empty village street, people went around and talked with each other as if they were visible. They stayed there because they had nowhere else to go. It was the middle of the day. Beneath us the ground was glowing, over us the sun burned.

2.

I arrived in Comala without luggage. Maybe the village had another name, I just don't know what. Names are winds that go by. I stood empty-handed under a dry tree which could have been one of the apple trees from my childhood. It was cold. Red didn't exist anymore.

3.

My father stood in front of me, dressed for Sunday as if he were going to a funeral. He held something in his hand which he gave to me. It was a gray apple covered in cold sweat.

4.

First when in death we achieve true equality. All dead are relatives. The ash is people who meet on the street corners to untangle their kinship ties. At last we are knitted together, I hear the one who loves say to the one who hates. At last, says the one who hates to the one who loves. In Comala, we speak so as not to expose our invisibility.

5.

There is a death after death. That's the one which happens when everyone has forgotten us.

A house in Granada

for Luis García Montero

1.

The house stood for a long time bolted
among surviving fruit trees.

No children laughed, no one sang,
no one dreamed anymore under the moon.

We approached at first carefully as thieves.
Was it the gold of oblivion we looked for?

A branch cracked ominously.
The leaves rustled, forbidden.

2.

A sense of guilt
was heavy as lead in the city.

No one knew what everyone knew,
and everyone hid what everyone knew

but said that they did not know.
That is why the house was bolted.

To be silent was another way
to murder someone already dead.

3.

… no quiero oír el llanto

Someone cries in the empty house.
Can others hear it?

The crying is a dry well,
it is grey, it is made of stone.

It has no eyes any longer,
and does not want to cry.

Can others hear it?
Someone cries in the empty house.

4.

The house was as if in another time,
where no uninitiated were allowed.

We approached with care.
Everything was silence and shadow there.

We were two witnesses who saw nothing
but wanted to see without being seen,

intruders under the moon,
the heavenly padlock.

5.

Did not the piano stand there,
left as someone mourning by a grave?

Did not dead flies lie in the window frame
as notes in a score?

Did not the empty flower vase
stand there like a decapitated angel?

And the wrinkled piece of paper in a corner:
The heart of the poet?

6.

Decades later. The city,
the old hypocrite had crawled closer

and was now lurking outside the gates.
The house appeared as before,

but now with open shutters.
Sky without clouds. Birds chirp

as in a recording from the twenties.
Was all already forgiven and forgotten?

7.

"The gentleman's imagery is not accurate,"
the museum docent seemed to imply.

"See for yourself, everything is neat,
the flies swept away,

the piano dusted,
the papers archived,

the frequency of visitors registered.
And the flowers scented as before."

8.

"No, not as before," I answered.
"As now." I showed my entrance ticket.

"Only the mind can visit
that which was before, not the senses.

Now when the moon jangles like coins
I would rather look for the shadow."

And I added:
"By the way: images are portals."

9.

The museum: the grave of the muse.

Critique of enthusiasm

(Managua revisited)

(In response to "The Grass of Managua")

1.

The place where I was
is the place where I am now.

A slope that begins in the blue
and ends in the American night

when the spotlights are turned off abruptly and people walk home.
The flags droop. The stage is empty.

Only one banderole left cries out:
"A vote for the president is a vote for God."

2.

On this slope the blasphemy
and the lie thus did meet.

The blasphemy said: "I am truth".
The lie said: "I am truth."

My friends saw no lie in the lie,
and thus did believe it.

I believed the blasphemy
or at least: the blasphemous thought.

3.

My friends turn away.
They are getting old, some of them are dead.

The have left their assignments.
They have renounced their portion of power.

That is why they know:
"The grass in Managua," they say,

"is nowadays gravel, and the gravel
can at the very most be used to make concrete."

4.

Those who reproach
the prophetic tone of my poem

are right, and so are they who blame me
for my imagery.

They are right concerning the palmistry
that I used: sentimental luster

that I deployed generously in order to please.
My only excuse is enthusiasm.

5.

"Enthusiasm," I heard them mumble.
"Enthusiasm was also ours,

but it leads nowhere.
To be enthusiastic is

to distance oneself, to go astray.
The reality is here." You can call it

the battlefield where things
that happen happen in shadow.

NOTES

"Farewell to childhood," is dedicated to Dennis Creffield (1931 – 2018), British artist.

"The poet writes for the wind," is dedicated to León Felipe (1884 – 1968), Spanish poet.

"The poet in April," mentions César Vallejo (1892 – 1938), Peruvian writer and poet.

"A small trip to heaven," dedicated to C.O. Hultén 1916 – 2015, Swedish artist.

"Five copper pennies," dedicated to Octavio Paz 1914 – 1998, Mexican writer and poet, Nobel Laureate.

"With Jorge Guillén," is about Jorge Guillén, 1893 – 1984, Spanish poet.

"Hunger," has an epigraph by Arthur Rimbaud, 1854 – 1891, French poet.

"When I walk through Jaffa Gate," has an epigraph by Dante Alighieri, 1265 – 1321, Italian poet.

"The crime was committed here," concerns Viznar, the village in Spain where the poet Federico García Lorca, (1898 – 1936) was killed.

"Cities," has an epigraph by Arthur Rimbaud, (1854-1891), French poet.

[I have worn my white linen shirt] mentions Fernando Pessoa, (1888 – 1935), Portuguese poet and novelist.

"The moon that Cervantes saw" takes place in Alcalá de Henares, the birthplace of Cervantes, (1547 – 1617), the author of Don Quixote.

"Mark Rothko" Mark Rothko, (1903 – 1970), Russian-American artist.

"To Jabes in Jerusalem" Edmond Jabès, French writer of Egyptian-Jewish origin.

"The one who knows nothing," part 13 mentionsLope de Vega, (1562 – 1635), Spanish poet and playwright.

"The one who knows nothing," part 18 mentions Luis Buñuel, (1900 – 1983), Spanish filmmaker and scriptwriter.

"The one who knows nothing," part 19 mentions Eli Lotar, (1905 – 1969), French photographer and cinematographer.

"With green ink," mentions Pablo Neruda, (1904 – 1973), Chilean poet.

"To Comala," refers to Comala, a ghost town in the novel Pedro Páramo by Mexican writer and photographer Juan Rulfo (1917 – 1986).

"A house in Granada" is dedicated to Luis García Montero, (b. 1958) Spanish poet.

"A house in Granada," part 3 includes an epigraph by Federico García Lorca.

ACKNOWLEDGEMENTS

We are grateful to the editors of *Poetry International* for publishing "Guyabera," "Organ grinder," "Sunset (Granada)," "The train stops," "(In my room at Mishkenot)," "The crime was committed here," "An Elegy," and "With Green Ink." The poem "(labyrinth)" appears in the Spring 2022 issue of *Ploughshares*, guest edited by Ilya Kaminsky.

The translators are grateful for the support of Lund University in Sweden and Georgetown University in the United States, which helped make our collaboration possible. We also thank Ángela Inés García Castrillón of Colombia and Sweden for bringing us all together on Världspoesidagen in Malmö, Sweden in 2017, an unforgettable gathering of poets. To Lasse Söderberg, our deepest gratitude, for entrusting us with your lyric art, and your confidence that we might find an American English where they might also be read and heard, as close to their original music as we could bring them.

Photo by Nils Sjöholm

Lars Gustaf Andersson is a poet and critic. He has translated works of British and American poets into Swedish, among them a selection of the poetry of Carolyn Forché, *Mot slutet* (Rámus 2020) and *Deaf Republic* by Ilya Kaminsky, *De dövas republik* (Rámus 2021). He is Professor of Film Studies at Lund University, Sweden, co-author of among others *Historical Dictionary of Scandinavian Cinema* (Scarecrow Press, 2012) and *The Cultural Practice of Immigrant Filmmaking* (Intellect Books, 2019). He lives in Lund with his wife Carina Sjöholm.

Carolyn Forché is a poet, memoirist, and translator. She is the author of the memoir *What You Have Heard Is True: A Memoir of Witness and Resistance* (Penguin Press, 2019), which was a finalist for the National Book Award, and five books of poetry. Her most recent poetry book, *In the Lateness of the World* (Penguin, 2020) was a finalist for the Pulitzer Prize. She is also editor of *Against Forgetting: Twentieth Century Poetry of Witness* (W.W. Norton, 1993) and co-editor of *Poetry of Witness: The Tradition in English 1500-2001*, with Duncan Wu (W.W. Norton, 2014). She has translated five books of poetry, most recently *America* by Fernando Valverde (Copper Canyon Press, 2021). She is University Professor at Georgetown University, and lives in Maryland with her husband, Harry Mattison.

Lasse Söderberg was born in 1931 in Stockholm, Sweden. He is the author of more than thirty books of poetry, and he is the foremost translator of post-war contemporary poets into Swedish from French, Spanish, Dutch, Danish, German, English, and Italian, including Octavio Paz, Yves Bonnefoy, Charles Simic, Jorge Luis Borges, André Breton, and Rafael Alberti. He founded International Poetry Days, a festival in Malmö, Sweden, and continues to arrange events in Malmö with his wife, Colombian poet Ángela García Ines Castrillon. He has received numerous awards for his poetry in Sweden and was named to an honorary professorship by the Swedish government in 2002. In 2019, he received the Max Jacob Prize in Paris. This is his first substantial volume in English.

Books by
ARROWSMITH
PRESS

Girls by Oksana Zabuzhko

Bula Matari/Smasher of Rocks by Tom Sleigh

This Carrying Life by Maureen McLane

Cries of Animal Dying by Lawrence Ferlinghetti

Animals in Wartime by Matiop Wal

Divided Mind by George Scialabba

The Jinn by Amira El-Zein

Bergstein
edited by Askold Melnyczuk

Arrow Breaking Apart by Jason Shinder

Beyond Alchemy by Daniel Berrigan

Conscience, Consequence: Reflections on Father Daniel Berrigan
edited by Askold Melnyczuk

Ric's Progress by Donald Hall

Return To The Sea by Etnairis Rivera

The Kingdom of His Will by Catherine Parnell

Eight Notes from the Blue Angel by Marjana Savka

Fifty-Two by Melissa Green

Music In—And On—The Air by Lloyd Schwartz

Magpiety by Melissa Green

Reality Hunger by William Pierce

Soundings: On The Poetry of Melissa Green
edited by Sumita Chakraborty

The Corny Toys by Thomas Sayers Ellis

Black Ops by Martin Edmunds

Museum of Silence by Romeo Oriogun

City of Water by Mitch Manning

Passeggiate by Judith Baumel

Persephone Blues by Oksana Lutsyshyna

The Uncollected Delmore Schwartz
edited by Ben Mazer

The Light Outside by George Kovach

The Blood of San Gennaro by Scott Harney
edited by Megan Marshall

No Sign by Peter Balakian

Firebird by Kythe Heller

The Selected Poems of Oksana Zabuzhko
edited by Askold Melnyczuk

The Age of Waiting by Douglas J. Penick

Manimal Woe by Fanny Howe

Crank Shaped Notes by Thomas Sayers Ellis

The Land of Mild Light by Rafael Cadenas
edited by Nidia Hernández

The Silence of Your Name by Alexandra Marshall

Flame in a Stable by Martin Edmunds

Mrs. Schmetterling by Robin Davidson

This Costly Season by John Okrent

Thorny by Judith Baumel

Some of You Will Know by David Rivard

www.ingramcontent.com/pod-product-compliance
Lightning Source LLC
Chambersburg PA
CBHW030249130626
46549CB00002B/454